Workbook

For

How to Not Die Alone

The Surprising Science That Will Help You Find Love

Max Prints

Copyright © 2024 Max Prints

All rights reserved. No part of this workbook may be reproduced, distributed, or transmitted in any form or by any means, including photocopying, recording, or other electronic or mechanical methods, without the prior written permission of the publisher, except in the case of brief quotations embodied in critical reviews and certain other noncommercial uses permitted by copyright law.

Table of Contents

How to Use This Workbook 6

Summary of the Book 10

SECTION 1: GETTING READY 14

Why Dating Is Harder Now Than Ever Before 14

    Key Lessons: 14

    Self-Reflection Questions: 16

The Three Dating Tendencies 20

    Key Lessons: 20

    Self-Reflection Questions: 21

Disney Lied to Us 24

    Key Lessons: 24

    Self-Reflection Questions: 25

Don't Let Perfect Be the Enemy of Great 28

    Key Lessons: 28

    Self-Reflection Questions: 29

Don't Wait, Date 32

Key Lessons: 32

Self-Reflection Questions: 33

Learn Your Attachment Style 36

Key Lessons: 36

Self-Reflection Questions: 38

Look for a Life Partner, Not a Prom Date 42

Key Lessons: 42

Self-Reflection Questions: 43

SECTION 2: GETTING OUT THERE 46

You Think You Know What You Want, but You're Wrong 46

Key Lessons: 46

Self-Reflection Questions: 47

Meet People IRL (In Real Life) 50

Key Lessons: 50

Self-Reflection Questions: 51

This Is a Date, Not a Job Interview 54

Key Lessons: 54

Self-Reflection Questions: 56

F**k the Spark **60**

Key Lessons: 60

Self-Reflection Questions: 61

Go on the Second Date **64**

Key Lessons: 64

Self-Reflection Questions: 65

SECTION 3: GETTING SERIOUS **68**

Decide, Don't Slide **68**

Key Lessons: 68

Self-Reflection Questions: 70

Stop Hitching and Stop Ditching **74**

Key Lessons: 74

Self-Reflection Questions: 76

Make a Breakup Plan **80**

Key Lessons: 80

Self-Reflection Questions: 82

Reframe Your Breakup as a Gain, Not a Loss **86**

Key Lessons: 86

Self-Reflection Questions: 88

Before You Tie the Knot, Do This **92**

Key Lessons: 92

Self-Reflection Questions: 93

Intentional love **96**

Key Lessons: 96

Self-Reflection Questions: 97

Self-Assessment Questions..**100**

How to Use This Workbook

1. Get Your Copy of How to Not Die Alone:

Before you dive into this companion workbook, make sure you have a copy of How to Not Die Alone. The workbook is designed to complement the book and provide exercises, prompts, and activities to reinforce your learning.

2. Read the Corresponding Chapter:

For each section of this workbook, there is a corresponding chapter in the main book. Start by reading the chapter in the book before moving on to the exercises in this workbook. This will help you grasp the core ideas and concepts before applying them.

3. Set Aside Dedicated Time:

Dedicate time to work on the exercises in this workbook. Find a quiet and comfortable space where you can focus without distractions. It's recommended to set aside time each day or week, depending on your schedule and goals.

4. Complete the Exercises:

Each section of this workbook contains a variety of exercises, prompts, and activities that are designed to deepen your understanding of the book's content. Take your time to complete them thoughtfully and honestly.

5. Reflect and Review:

After completing an exercise or activity, take a moment to reflect on your answers or insights. This self-reflection is essential for personal growth and development. You may even want to review and revisit your responses periodically to track your progress.

6. Share Your Insights:

Consider discussing your thoughts and experiences with a friend, a study group, or an online community. Sharing your insights can lead to valuable discussions and provide additional perspectives on the book's content.

7. Keep a Journal:

Many of the exercises in this workbook encourage you to keep a journal. Consider starting a journal specifically for your reflections on the book's content and your progress with the workbook.

8. Take Action:

The book and this companion workbook are meant to inspire change and action. As you work through the exercises, identify specific actions you can take to apply the book's principles in your daily life.

9. Track Your Progress:

Use the provided tracking pages to monitor your progress and achievements as you work through the workbook. Celebrate your successes, no matter how small they may seem.

10. Enjoy the Journey:

Finally, remember that personal growth is a journey. Don't rush through the workbook; take your time to absorb the knowledge and implement the changes you wish to see in your life.

This companion workbook is your guide to applying the wisdom of "How to Not Die Alone" to your life. Use it as a tool for personal growth, and most importantly, enjoy the process of learning and self-discovery. We wish you a transformative and fulfilling experience with both the book and this workbook.

Summary of the Book

Love can feel like a mystical force, sweeping us off our feet without rhyme or reason. But Logan Ury, a behavioral scientist turned dating coach, begs to differ in her book "How to Not Die Alone: The Surprising Science That Will Help You Find Love." She argues that finding lasting love isn't about serendipity, it's about making smart choices backed by science.

Unmasking Our Dating Biases:
The book starts by dismantling common myths and exposing our unconscious biases that sabotage our love lives. We learn about three common dating tendencies:

Maximizers: Always seeking the "best" option, leading to chronic indecision and missed opportunities.

Romanticizers: Chasing the fairy tale ideal, often overlooking red flags in pursuit of fantasy.

Hesitaters: Fearful of commitment, prone to self-sabotage and avoiding vulnerability.

Ury identifies our attachment styles, ingrained patterns of relating formed in childhood, as another crucial factor. Anxious attachers crave constant reassurance, avoidants push intimacy away, and secure attachers navigate relationships with ease. Understanding your style can help you avoid unhealthy dynamics.

Building a Better Dating Strategy:

Once we've identified our blind spots, Ury equips us with actionable tools to transform our dating lives. She emphasizes the importance of intentional love, actively creating the relationship you desire rather than passively hoping for the best. This involves setting clear goals, crafting an attractive online profile, and approaching dates with curiosity and open communication.

The book delves into the nitty-gritty of online dating, offering tips on crafting compelling bios, navigating the initial message exchange, and making the most of first dates. Ury emphasizes the importance of filtering for compatibility, seeking partners who share your values and life goals.

Nurturing a Thriving Relationship:

But finding the right person is just the beginning. Ury guides us through the crucial stages of building a strong, lasting relationship. She emphasizes the power of vulnerability and authenticity, encouraging us to share our true selves and embrace genuine emotional connection.

Effective communication is key, and Ury provides tools for navigating conflict constructively, expressing needs assertively, and building trust. She also highlights the importance of maintaining emotional intelligence, understanding and managing our own emotions to foster healthy interactions.

Beyond the Binary:

"How to Not Die Alone" challenges the "one true love" myth, reminding us that multiple fulfilling relationships are possible throughout life. The book also addresses LGBTQ+ experiences and offers inclusive advice for navigating the dating world with authenticity.

A Science-backed Roadmap to Love:
Ury's book is a treasure trove of practical advice grounded in scientific research. It's a refreshing antidote to romantic cliches, empowering us to take control of our love lives with intentionality and self-awareness. Whether you're a seasoned dater or just starting out, "How to Not Die Alone" offers valuable insights and tools to guide you on your journey to finding lasting love.

Remember, the key takeaway is that love is a choice, not a chance. By understanding our biases, making smart decisions, and nurturing healthy relationships, we can all increase our chances of finding the love we deserve.

So, ditch the fairytales and grab a copy of "How to Not Die Alone." With its blend of humor, science, and practical advice, it might just be the roadmap you need to navigate the exciting, sometimes messy, but ultimately rewarding world of love.

SECTION 1: GETTING READY

Why Dating Is Harder Now Than Ever Before

Key Lessons:

1. Shifting Identity Landscape: In today's world, individuals define themselves more than ever before, unlike past generations where community played a major role. This independence makes finding a compatible partner who complements, not completes, your identity much more complex.

2. Paradox of Choice: Dating apps and platforms offer an abundance of potential partners, leading to "decision fatigue" and questioning every choice. This makes it harder to commit and build meaningful connections amid the constant temptation of "what if."

3. Social Media Mirage: Online platforms often portray relationships as idealized and effortless, causing

unrealistic expectations and feelings of inadequacy in real-life dating experiences. This negativity bias can further discourage active engagement and vulnerability.

Self-Reflection Questions:

1. How has your evolving identity influenced your approach to dating and relationships? Do you seek partners who complement your self-concept or try to fill perceived gaps?

_____

_____

_____

_____

2. In the face of endless dating options, how do you manage decision fatigue and avoid falling into the trap of constantly comparing potential partners? What strategies help you focus on genuine connection and building relationships?

_____

_____

_____

_____

3. How aware are you of the potentially misleading portrayal of relationships on social media? How does this influence your expectations and experiences in real-world dating? What steps can you take to manage these influences and stay grounded in reality?

_____

_____

_____

_____

_____

4. Despite the challenges discussed, what motivates you to pursue love and meaningful connection? What personal strengths and values can you leverage to navigate the modern dating landscape effectively?

_____

_____

_____

_____

Remember, these are just prompts to get you started. Feel free to explore these questions further and delve deeper into your own experiences and perspectives.

The Three Dating Tendencies

Key Lessons:

1. Dating blind spots exist: We all have tendencies that skew our dating behavior, often unconsciously. Identifying these tendencies, like romanticizing partners or over-focusing on finding "the one," is crucial for successful dating.

2. Breaking free from Tendencies: Each tendency has specific strategies to overcome it. Romanticizers need to focus on reality, Maximizers on taking risks, and Hesitators on proactive action.

3. Balance is key: No tendency is inherently bad. The goal is to find a healthy balance where your natural patterns don't hinder your ability to build fulfilling relationships.

Self-Reflection Questions:

1. Which tendency resonates most with you? Consider past and present dating experiences. Do you find yourself idealizing partners, seeking endless options, or delaying action?

_____
_____
_____
_____
_____

2. How has your tendency impacted your past relationships? Reflect on how your dominant tendency might have sabotaged past connections or influenced your choices.

_____
_____
_____
_____
_____

3. What specific examples of your tendency can you identify? Recall concrete situations where your tendency manifested, hindering healthy connection or decision-making.

___

___

___

___

___

4. What action steps can you take to counter your tendency? Based on the strategies Ury suggests for your identified tendency, brainstorm specific actions you can implement in your dating life.

___

___

___

___

___

___

Remember, self-awareness is key to navigating the dating world. By understanding your tendencies and actively counteracting their negative influence, you can move towards building healthier and more fulfilling relationships.

Disney Lied to Us

Key Lessons:

1. Love isn't passive or magical: Forget the prince charming swooping in. Finding love takes active effort, intentionality, and putting yourself out there. Waiting for "fate" might leave you waiting forever.

2. Passion fades, but compatibility builds: That initial intense spark is exciting, but it wanes over time. True lasting love is built on shared values, communication, and compatibility, which deepen with effort and shared experiences.

3. Relationships require work, not just magic: Disney paints relationships as effortless fairytale bliss. In reality, healthy partnerships require compromise, communication, and ongoing effort from both partners. It's a journey, not a destination.

Self-Reflection Questions:

1. How have Disney and other media shaped your expectations for love? Do these expectations align with reality or set you up for disappointment? How can you adjust your perception of love for a healthier approach?

_____
_____
_____
_____
_____

2. What are your relationship dealbreakers? Separate genuine incompatibilities from superficial preferences. Can you learn to compromise on certain things for someone compatible in the long run?

_____
_____
_____
_____
_____

3. Are you actively putting yourself out there to meet potential partners? Are you relying on chance encounters or making a genuine effort to expand your social circle and engage in activities where you might meet someone compatible?

___

4. Are you willing to invest time and effort into building a foundation for a lasting relationship? Are you prepared to nurture communication, compromise, and growth? Remember, love is a verb, not just a feeling.

___

By reflecting on these lessons and questions, you can gain a more realistic and grounded perspective on love and set yourself up for success in finding truly fulfilling relationships.

Remember, there's no magic wand, but there's a treasure trove of knowledge and effort that can guide you on a more fulfilling journey towards love.

Don't Let Perfect Be the Enemy of Great

Key Lessons:

1. Perfectionism Paralysis: Striving for an unrealistically perfect partner or relationship can lead to inaction and missed opportunities. Remember, great relationships are built, not discovered.

2. Progress over Perfection: Taking imperfect steps, like putting yourself out there or initiating dates, is far more valuable than waiting for everything to be flawless. Focus on making progress, not achieving perfection.

3. Vulnerability as Strength: Sharing your true self, flaws and all, fosters genuine connections and deeper intimacy. Embrace vulnerability as a pathway to stronger, more fulfilling relationships.

Self-Reflection Questions:

1. How often do you allow the pursuit of perfection to prevent you from taking risks in your dating life? Identify specific situations where perfectionism held you back and brainstorm alternative approaches.

_____

_____

_____

_____

_____

2. What small, actionable steps can you take to put yourself out there more, even if imperfectly? Consider joining a club, online dating platforms, or simply striking up conversations with new people.

_____

_____

_____

_____

3. In what ways can you be more vulnerable and authentic in your interactions with potential partners? Reflect on areas where you hold back or mask your true self, and explore ways to share your genuine thoughts and feelings.

_____
_____
_____
_____
_____

4. How can you challenge your own negative self-talk and embrace your imperfections? Practice self-compassion, reframe negative thoughts into positive affirmations, and celebrate your unique qualities.

_____
_____
_____
_____
_____

Remember, the path to love is rarely linear or perfect. By letting go of perfectionism, taking action, and embracing vulnerability, you open yourself up to more fulfilling connections and ultimately, a happier love life.

Don't Wait, Date

Key Lessons:

1. Proactiveness beats patience: Waiting passively for love rarely works. The chapter argues that actively putting yourself out there, even if it feels uncomfortable, significantly increases your chances of finding a romantic partner.

2. Reframe rejection: Don't see rejection as a personal failure. Instead, view it as a data point in your search for compatibility. Every "no" brings you closer to the "yes" you seek.

3. Quantity leads to quality: Contrary to popular belief, dating more people initially can actually help you refine your preferences and identify what truly matters in a partner. This broader experience ultimately guides you towards more fulfilling connections.

Self-Reflection Questions:

1. What are your current dating habits? How proactive are you in seeking potential partners? Do you rely primarily on chance encounters or actively make an effort to meet new people?

_____

_____

_____

_____

_____

2. How do you typically react to rejection? Do you allow it to discourage you or do you see it as an opportunity for learning and growth?

_____

_____

_____

_____

_____

3. Have you clearly defined your priorities in a potential partner? What qualities and values are most important to you in a long-term relationship?

_____

_____

_____

_____

_____

4. Are you willing to step outside your comfort zone and explore new dating avenues? This could involve trying online dating platforms, attending social events you wouldn't normally go to, or initiating conversations with potential partners.

_____

_____

_____

_____

_____

Remember, the goal is to be honest with yourself and identify areas where you might be holding yourself back. Embrace a growth mindset and see these questions as a starting point for your own unique journey towards finding love.

Learn Your Attachment Style

Key Lessons:

1. Attachment Matters: Understanding your attachment style, a blueprint for how you bond in relationships, is crucial for navigating romantic connections more effectively. It unveils patterns in your behavior and helps you explain why certain dynamics feel familiar or frustrating.

2. Early Roots, Lasting Impact: Attachment styles are shaped in early childhood, primarily through interactions with caregivers. These experiences lay the foundation for how you seek closeness, communicate needs, and handle conflict in adult relationships.

3. Four Styles, Four Stories: There are four main attachment styles: secure, anxious, avoidant, and disorganized. Each style reflects a distinct pattern of relating, with secure individuals exhibiting healthy emotional balance, anxious individuals craving constant reassurance, avoidant individuals preferring emotional

distance, and disorganized individuals struggling with inconsistent attachment patterns.

Self-Reflection Questions:

1. Relationship Rhythm: Reflect on your typical behavior in close relationships. Do you seek frequent intimacy and communication (anxious), value independence and avoid enmeshment (avoidant), find comfort in a balanced give-and-take (secure), or experience unpredictable emotional engagement (disorganized)?

_____

_____

_____

2. Childhood Echoes: Consider any significant experiences in your childhood that might have influenced your attachment style. Did you have reliable caregivers who were emotionally available and responsive? Were there periods of separation or inconsistency in your early relationships?

_____

_____

_____

3. Relationship Patterns: Identify any recurring patterns in your romantic relationships. Do you find yourself in one-sided dynamics, constantly seeking validation, pushing partners away, or struggling with trust and commitment? How might understanding your attachment style explain these patterns?

_____

_____

_____

4. Cultivating Secure Connection: Recognizing your attachment style is the first step towards fostering healthier relationship dynamics. What conscious efforts can you make to build a more secure attachment style in your future relationships, such as practicing open communication, setting healthy boundaries, and prioritizing emotional stability?

_____

_____

_____

_____

Remember, understanding your attachment style is not about assigning blame or seeking excuses. It's a powerful tool for self-awareness and growth, allowing you to build more fulfilling and lasting connections.

Look for a Life Partner, Not a Prom Date

Key Lessons:

1. Shift your focus from short-term attraction to long-term compatibility. We tend to prioritize spark and initial excitement, which fades and can lead to disappointment. Instead, seek partners with shared values, life goals, and complementary communication styles.

2. Ditch the "checklist mentality." While having dealbreakers is important, rigid lists can overlook wonderful connections that don't tick every box. Focus on understanding someone's character, values, and how they make you feel rather than superficial traits.

3. Build genuine intimacy through vulnerability and communication. Go beyond surface-level conversations and share your hopes, fears, and vulnerabilities. Honest communication, active listening, and open sharing are crucial for building trust and emotional connection.

Self-Reflection Questions:

1. What qualities and values are truly essential for you in a long-term partner? Prioritize these over short-term excitement or superficial traits.

_____

_____

_____

_____

_____

2. Do you tend to overlook potential partners who don't perfectly fit your "checklist"? Consider giving someone a chance if they align with your core values and offer genuine emotional connection.

_____

_____

_____

_____

_____

3. How comfortable are you sharing your vulnerabilities and truly connecting on a deeper level? Practice open communication and be willing to take emotional risks in your relationships.

_____
_____
_____
_____
_____

4. Think about past relationships where you prioritized attraction over compatibility. What did you learn from those experiences? Apply those lessons to your current and future dating approach.

_____
_____
_____
_____
_____

By reflecting on these lessons and questions, you can shift your perspective from seeking a temporary thrill to finding a true and lasting partner for life.

SECTION 2: GETTING OUT THERE

You Think You Know What You Want, but You're Wrong

Key Lessons:

1. Your "must-haves" might be sabotaging you: Rigid criteria based on idealized expectations, often influenced by media and societal norms, can blind you to compatible partners who don't tick every box.

2. Real love is built, not found: The "soulmate" fantasy ignores the importance of shared experiences, compromise, and deliberate effort in growing a lasting connection.

3. Focus on values, not dealbreakers: Prioritize shared values that align with your long-term vision for a fulfilling life, rather than fixating on superficial qualities or temporary dealbreakers.

Self-Reflection Questions:

1. Have you held onto any "must-have" qualities in a partner that might be narrowing your dating pool unnecessarily? Can you reframe these as preferences while prioritizing core values compatibility?

_____
_____
_____
_____
_____

2. Do you tend to romanticize the initial spark as a predictor of long-term success, overlooking the importance of building a deeper connection with someone over time?

_____
_____
_____
_____

3. Can you identify any dealbreakers that might be based on personal biases or fleeting desires, rather than fundamental incompatibilities with your long-term aspirations?

_____
_____
_____
_____
_____
_____

4. What are your core values in life? How can you actively seek potential partners who share these values and support your overall vision for fulfillment?

_____
_____
_____
_____
_____
_____

Remember, the answers to these questions are personal and there's no right or wrong. The goal is to gain self-awareness and challenge any limiting beliefs or patterns that might be hindering your journey towards lasting love.

Meet People IRL (In Real Life)

Key Lessons:

1. Expand Your Circles Beyond Apps: Apps are handy, but they limit your pool to a specific algorithm. Break free by trying social groups, hobbies, volunteering, or simply striking up conversations at everyday places like coffee shops or parks.

2. Rejection is Inevitable, Embrace It: Fear of rejection often cripples dating efforts. Remember, not everyone clicks, and that's okay. View rejection as learning experiences, not failures. Each "no" brings you closer to a "yes."

3. Master the Art of Initiating Interactions: Don't wait for someone to approach you. Take charge! Ask open-ended questions, use active listening, and share genuine interests. Show people you're genuinely interested in connecting.

Self-Reflection Questions:

1. What one new activity or group activity could you try in the next month to meet potential partners outside of dating apps?

_____

_____

_____

_____

_____

_____

2. What negative thought patterns come up when you face rejection? How can you reframe these thoughts to be more positive and encouraging?

_____

_____

_____

_____

_____

3. Think about someone you find interesting in your daily life (coworker, barista, etc.). What small step could you take to initiate a conversation with them?

_____
_____
_____
_____
_____
_____

4. Are there any social skills you feel could be improved to make you more comfortable meeting people in real life? How can you practice and develop these skills?

_____
_____
_____
_____
_____
_____

Remember, finding love often requires stepping outside your comfort zone and actively putting yourself out there. Use these lessons and questions to get started on your journey to meaningful connections!

This Is a Date, Not a Job Interview

Key Lessons:

1. Shift from performance to connection: Dates shouldn't be about proving yourself or impressing your partner. Instead, focus on creating a genuine connection by asking open-ended questions, actively listening, and sharing authentically about yourself.

2. Embrace vulnerability and curiosity: Don't be afraid to show your genuine curiosity about your date and share some vulnerabilities (not TMI, of course) to foster deeper connection. This vulnerability creates a safe space for your date to reciprocate and allows you to see beyond the surface.

3. Focus on present enjoyment, not future potential: Avoid getting caught up in analyzing your date's potential as a long-term partner. Be present in the moment, enjoy the conversation and their company, and

let the connection unfold naturally. Overanalyzing too early can cloud your judgment and prevent you from seeing someone for who they really are.

Self-Reflection Questions:

1. Do you tend to approach dates with a "performance mindset" focused on impressing your date? How can you shift your focus to creating a genuine connection instead?

_____
_____
_____
_____
_____
_____

2. What are some ways you can practice vulnerability and show genuine interest in your date beyond the typical "get-to-know-you" questions?

_____
_____
_____
_____
_____
_____

3. Do you find yourself analyzing your date's potential for a long-term relationship too early on? How can you stay present in the moment and enjoy the experience without jumping to conclusions?

_____

_____

_____

_____

_____

4. Think about past dates where you may have approached things from a "job interview" perspective. What did you learn from those experiences, and how can you apply that knowledge to future dates?

_____

_____

_____

_____

_____

_____

Remember, the goal of dating is to find someone you click with and enjoy spending time with, not to land a perfect partner. By shifting your mindset and focusing on connection, you'll open yourself up to more fulfilling dating experiences.

F**k the Spark

Key Lessons:

1. Love Isn't Magic: The initial "spark" is often a chemical cocktail that fades quickly. True love takes time, effort, and shared experiences to build.

2. Compatibility Matters More Than Chemistry: Shared values, goals, and communication styles are crucial for long-term compatibility. Focus on these instead of chasing fleeting excitement.

3. Vulnerability Breeds Connection: Opening up about vulnerabilities fosters trust and intimacy, creating a deeper bond than superficial attraction.

Self-Reflection Questions:

1. How much weight have you given to the "spark" in past relationships? Has it always led to successful connections?

_____

_____

_____

_____

_____

_____

2. What are your core values and goals in a relationship? Do you actively seek partners who share these?

_____

_____

_____

_____

_____

_____

3. Think of a close friend or family member. What makes your connection strong? Can you apply these qualities to romantic relationships?

_____

_____

_____

_____

_____

_____

4. Are you comfortable being vulnerable with potential partners? What steps could you take to open up more effectively?

_____

_____

_____

_____

_____

_____

Remember, "F**k the Spark" encourages a shift in perspective. True love takes work, but the rewards of a genuine, enduring connection far outweigh the fleeting rush of initial attraction.

I hope these lessons and questions spark some insightful reflection!

Go on the Second Date

Key Lessons:

1. Second dates reveal more than first dates: The initial spark can be misleading. A second date provides a deeper layer of information about compatibility, shared values, and long-term potential. Don't write someone off after just one encounter.

2. Focus on curiosity, not certainty: Approach the second date with an open mind and genuine interest in learning more about the person. Ask questions, actively listen, and be observant. Ditch the pressure to find "the one" and enjoy getting to know someone new.

3. Beyond the butterflies: Look for shared values and growth potential: While attraction is important, it's not sustainable alone. Pay attention to shared values, communication styles, and future goals. Can you envision building a meaningful life together? Are you both open to personal growth and compromise?

Self-Reflection Questions:

1. Have you rushed to judgment based on a single date? Has fear of missing out or the thrill of the chase ever led you to dismiss someone prematurely? Remember, second dates offer a clearer picture.

_____

_____

_____

_____

_____

2. What are your non-negotiables in a partner? Define your core values and dealbreakers before entering a new relationship. This clarity will guide your decisions and prevent wasted time.

_____

_____

_____

_____

3. Are you a good listener? Do you ask follow-up questions and truly engage in what the other person is saying? Effective communication is crucial for building trust and understanding.

_____
_____
_____
_____
_____

4. Can you differentiate between sparks and substance? Do you mistake initial excitement for genuine compatibility? Be mindful of your tendency to romanticize and focus on building a foundation of shared values instead of fleeting butterflies.

_____
_____
_____
_____

By reflecting on these lessons and questions, you can approach second dates with greater intention and understanding, setting yourself up for more fulfilling connections. Remember, finding love is a journey, not a destination. Enjoy the process and let curiosity guide you!

SECTION 3: GETTING SERIOUS

Decide, Don't Slide

Key Lessons:

1. Consciously Navigating Milestones: Relationships don't just happen, they progress through intentional decisions. Actively consider where you stand - are you exclusive? Is this heading towards something serious? Don't let ambiguity fester; open communication about expectations lays the foundation for a healthy relationship.

2. Breaking the Slide Habit: Passively allowing relationships to drift can lead to disappointment and confusion. Instead, make decisive choices about who you spend time with and invest in. Avoid falling into autopilot; actively choose to pursue or step away from connections that align with your goals and values.

3. Communicating with Clarity: Fear of awkwardness or rejection often leads to vague conversations about relationship status. Be brave! Initiate honest discussions about expectations and feelings. Clear communication avoids misunderstandings and allows both partners to make informed decisions about the future.

Self-Reflection Questions:

1. Do you tend to "slide" in relationships, avoiding crucial conversations about commitment and expectations? Why or why not?

_____
_____
_____
_____
_____
_____

2. In your past relationships, have you ever experienced confusion or resentment due to a lack of clarity about commitment? What could you have done differently?

_____
_____
_____
_____
_____
_____

3. Identify one upcoming relationship milestone (exclusivity, moving in, etc.). How can you prepare to have a clear and confident conversation about it?

_____
_____
_____
_____
_____
_____

4. What are your personal values and goals in a relationship? How can actively choosing partners and situations aligned with these values benefit your dating life?

_____
_____
_____
_____
_____
_____

Remember, taking the time to reflect on these questions can empower you to navigate relationships with intention and clarity, setting yourself up for more fulfilling connections.

Stop Hitching and Stop Ditching

Key Lessons:

1. Awareness of Relationship Patterns: This chapter highlights the importance of acknowledging your tendencies in relationships. Do you jump from partner to partner without taking time to reflect (hitching)? Or do you quickly bail once things get challenging (ditching)? Recognizing these patterns empowers you to make conscious choices instead of acting instinctively.

2. Effective Breakup Strategies: Breaking up doesn't have to be messy or hurtful. The chapter emphasizes using clear communication, empathy, and taking responsibility for your part in the relationship. This approach allows for closure and potentially preserves future friendships.

3. Navigating Uncertainty: Dating often involves navigating ambiguity and unfamiliarity. Ury encourages embracing this uncertainty rather than seeking immediate

security or clarity. Learning to be comfortable with the unknown opens doors to deeper connections and personal growth.

Self-Reflection Questions:

1. Hitching or Ditching?: Honestly evaluate your past and current relationships. Have you exhibited patterns of quickly moving on or impulsively ending things? What factors might be driving these tendencies?

_____

_____

_____

_____

2. Communication Crossroads: When faced with potential conflict or challenges in a relationship, how do you typically communicate? Do you avoid difficult conversations or express your needs assertively? Consider strategies for navigating disagreements in a healthy and productive manner.

_____

_____

_____

3. Comfort in the Unknown: Can you tolerate ambiguity and uncertainty in your dating life, or do you constantly seek immediate reassurance and commitment? Explore what fears or anxieties might be hindering your ability to embrace the natural ebb and flow of relationships.

_____

_____

_____

_____

4. Intentional Growth: What steps can you take to move beyond your habitual relationship patterns and build more fulfilling connections? Do you need to develop better communication skills, practice vulnerability, or learn to let go of expectations? Commit to intentional growth and self-improvement for a more rewarding dating experience.

_____

_____

_____

_____

Remember, these questions are prompts for personal reflection. There are no right or wrong answers, and the most important takeaway is to gain insights into your own relationship dynamics and make choices that align with your values and goals.

Make a Breakup Plan

Key Lessons:

1. Clarity over Chaos: Endings deserve planning just like beginnings. A breakup plan provides clarity and structure during an emotionally charged time, minimizing impulsiveness and maximizing self-respect. It allows you to communicate your decision with honesty and compassion, even if the relationship wasn't healthy.

2. Focus on the "Why": Before "how," understand the "why" behind your decision. Reflect on your needs, values, and goals. Are you unhappy? Unfulfilled? Is the relationship hindering your growth? By identifying the core reasons, you gain conviction and avoid the temptation to rekindle the relationship based on fleeting emotions.

3. Compassionate Communication: Breakups don't have to be brutal. Plan a conversation that acknowledges the other person's feelings while assertively stating your own. Choose a neutral location, practice what you want

to say beforehand, and focus on "I" statements to avoid blame. Remember, kindness and honesty go a long way, even in difficult situations.

Self-Reflection Questions:

1. What are your dealbreakers in a relationship? Reflect on the non-negotiable values and needs that must be met for a relationship to thrive. This clarity will guide your future partner selection and help you recognize when it's time to let go.

_____

_____

_____

_____

2. Have you communicated your needs effectively in this relationship? Did you give your partner a chance to understand your concerns and adjust their behavior? Open communication can sometimes mend issues before reaching a breaking point.

_____

_____

_____

_____

3. Are you holding onto the relationship out of fear of being alone? Remember, being single is not a failure. It's an opportunity for self-discovery and growth. Prioritize your happiness and well-being above the fear of solitude.

_____
_____
_____
_____
_____

4. What do you hope to gain from this breakup? Is it personal growth, clarity for future relationships, or simply emotional freedom? Identifying your desired outcome will motivate you through the transition and help you focus on positive steps forward.

_____
_____
_____
_____
_____

Remember, breakups are often painful but necessary chapters in our lives. By approaching them with intention and self-reflection, you can navigate them with dignity and pave the way for a fulfilling future.

Reframe Your Breakup as a Gain, Not a Loss

Key Lessons:

1. Growth through Breakups: Reframe breakups as opportunities for personal growth. Just like challenges and failures, they provide valuable life lessons that can strengthen your emotional intelligence, communication skills, and self-awareness. This newfound knowledge enhances your future relationships and makes you a better partner.

2. Rediscovering Yourself: Breakups allow you to reconnect with your individual needs and desires. Reflect on what matters most to you, your passions, and values. Without the demands of a relationship, you have the freedom to explore new interests, reconnect with friends, and prioritize self-care. This period of solo rediscovery fosters a deeper understanding of yourself, setting a strong foundation for future partnerships.

3. Shifting Perspective: Don't view breakups solely as losses. Acknowledge the positive aspects that emerge. You gain independence, free time, and the chance to rebuild your social circle. Appreciate the closure they bring, ending an incompatible relationship and freeing you to pursue a more fulfilling connection.

Self-Reflection Questions:

1. What valuable lessons have you learned from past breakups that have strengthened you and your relationships?

_____

_____

_____

_____

_____

_____

2. Outside of a relationship, what activities bring you joy and fulfillment? How can you prioritize these in your current life?

_____

_____

_____

_____

_____

3. What are your non-negotiable values and needs in a partner? How can understanding these guide you in future relationships?

_____
_____
_____
_____
_____
_____
_____

4. What positive aspects have emerged from your recent breakup? How can you leverage these strengths and newfound freedom to move forward?

_____
_____
_____
_____
_____
_____
_____

Remember, the goal is not to erase the pain of your breakup but to utilize it as a catalyst for growth and self-discovery. By reframing your perspective and focusing on the positive, you can navigate this challenging time and emerge stronger, better prepared for the fulfilling relationship you deserve.

Before You Tie the Knot, Do This

Key Lessons:

1. Self-awareness is crucial: Before committing to marriage, understanding your own values, goals, and dealbreakers is essential. This chapter might encourage examining personal growth areas, communication styles, and desired dynamics in a long-term partnership.

2. Intentional communication is key: Effective communication goes beyond casual conversation. This lesson could emphasize the importance of clear and honest communication about expectations, needs, and potential challenges within a marriage.

3. Shared values and goals matter: Compatibility might extend beyond surface-level interests. This chapter may explore the importance of aligning on core values, life goals, and visions for the future as a couple.

Self-Reflection Questions:

1. What are your non-negotiables in a long-term partnership? What values, habits, or qualities are absolutely essential for your happiness and well-being in a marriage?

___

___

___

___

___

2. How comfortable are you communicating effectively about difficult topics or potential conflicts? Do you tend to avoid tough conversations, or can you approach them openly and constructively?

___

___

___

___

3. To what extent do your long-term goals and aspirations align with those of your partner? Are you both on the same page about career paths, family desires, and financial priorities?

_____

_____

_____

_____

_____

4. What areas of personal growth do you feel are important to address before potentially entering a marriage? Are there emotional vulnerabilities, communication patterns, or life skills you'd like to work on before taking the next step?

_____

_____

_____

_____

Remember, these are just potential lessons and questions based on the chapter title and my understanding of the book's theme. It's always best to read the chapter yourself for a complete and accurate understanding of Ury's advice.

I hope this helps! Let me know if you have any other questions.

Intentional love

Key Lessons:

1. Shifting Gears: Move from passively "finding" love to actively creating it through deliberate actions and behaviors. This means approaching dating with intentionality, setting clear goals, and taking concrete steps to build meaningful connections.

2. Vulnerability Matters: Strong, lasting relationships thrive on vulnerability and authenticity. Share your true self, express your needs and desires openly, and don't shy away from genuine emotional connection. Remember, intimacy blooms where walls come down.

3. EQ is Key: Develop your emotional intelligence to understand and manage your own emotions effectively. This includes self-awareness, recognizing your triggers, and navigating conflict constructively. Strong emotional intelligence fosters healthier, more fulfilling relationships.

Self-Reflection Questions:

1. Cultivating Attraction: What qualities and behaviors can you actively cultivate to attract the kind of love you seek? How can you embody these qualities in your interactions and dating approach?

_____

_____

_____

_____

_____

2. Vulnerability in Action: In what ways can you practice greater vulnerability and authenticity in your daily life and romantic connections? Are there areas where you hold back that could deepen your relationships?

_____

_____

_____

_____

_____

3. Boosting EQ: What steps can you take to improve your emotional intelligence? Consider exploring resources, practicing mindfulness, or seeking support to better understand and manage your emotions.

_____

_____

_____

_____

_____

4. Intentional vs. Passive: Do you currently approach dating with an intentional mindset focused on creating love, or do you find yourself passively waiting for it to happen? How can you shift your perspective and take an active role in shaping your romantic future?

_____

_____

_____

_____

_____

Remember, these are just starting points. As you delve deeper into "Intentional Love," you'll discover a wealth of insights and practical tools to guide you on your journey to creating fulfilling, lasting relationships.

Self-Assessment Questions

1. Did you achieve all of your goals for this workbook, and if not, what prevented you from doing so?

_____
_____
_____
_____
_____
_____

2. What were the most significant challenges you encountered during the workbook, and how did you address them?

_____
_____
_____
_____
_____
_____

3. How well did you manage your time and resources throughout the workbook? Were there any areas where you could have been more efficient?

_____
_____
_____
_____
_____
_____
_____

4. Have You effectively applied the knowledge and skills gained in this workbook to your personal or professional life?

_____
_____
_____
_____
_____
_____
_____

5. Can you identify specific areas of improvement or growth that have occurred in yourself as a result of completing this workbook?

_____
_____
_____
_____
_____
_____

6. Did you seek help or collaborate with others when facing difficulties, and if so, how did this impact the overall outcome of your workbook experience?

_____
_____
_____
_____
_____
_____

7. What strategies did you employ to stay motivated and focused on completing the tasks and assignments in this workbook?

_____
_____
_____
_____
_____
_____

8. Were there any moments when you felt overwhelmed or disengaged, and what steps did you take to regain your momentum?

_____
_____
_____
_____
_____
_____

9. Have you kept track of your progress and accomplishments throughout the workbook, and do you feel satisfied with what you've achieved?

_____

_____

_____

_____

_____

10. Looking ahead, what are your future plans for applying the knowledge and skills gained from this workbook in your ongoing personal or professional development?

_____

_____

_____

_____

_____

_____

These questions can help you reflect on your workbook experience and assess your progress objectively.

Made in the USA
Columbia, SC
19 May 2024

35894470R00065